DEDICATION

This book is dedicated to all those who strive
tirelessly to understand themselves better and who
have the courage to change, grow, and embrace
every aspect of life with an open heart and mind. It
is for the seekers of wisdom, the pursuers of growth,
and the champions of personal transformation.
May this work inspire you to continue your journey
with resilience, courage, and an enduring sense of
wonder. May it serve as a guide and companion in
your quest for a deeper understanding and a fuller,
more rewarding life.

ᚦᚦᚦ

THE SCIENCE OF EMPOWERING THE SELF

NAVIGATING LIFE'S CHALLENGES WITH PSYCHOLOGICAL WISDOM

DR. MINAKSHI BANSAL

Contents

Contents

Prayer

"Om Bhadram Karnebhih Shrinuyama Devah
Bhadram Pashyemakshabhiryajatrah
Sthirairangais Tushtuvamsastanubhih
Vyashema Devahitam Yadayuh
Svasti Na Indro Vriddhashravah
Svasti Nah Pusha Vishwavedah
Svasti Nastarkshyo Arishtanemih
Svasti No Brihaspatir Dadhatu
Om Shantih Shantih Shantih"

This mantra is a prayer for universal well-being, invoking the blessings of various deities for protection, health, and happiness. It emphasizes the importance of experiencing the auspicious through all senses and living a life aligned with divine purpose. The repetition of "Shantih" at the end signifies a deep desire for peace in the individual, the environment, and the universe at large. This mantra is often recited as a prayer for peace, prosperity, and the physical and spiritual well-being of all beings.

About The Author

Dr. Minakshi Bansal, born in the bustling metropolis of Delhi, India, has led a life steeped in artistry, scholarly pursuit, and an unwavering commitment to societal betterment. Following her marriage, she relocated to Ahmedabad, Gujarat, where she has since blossomed into a multifaceted beacon of inspiration for many. Dr. Minakshi is not only recognized as a gifted artist in the realm of Fine Arts but also as an esteemed author, a devoted social worker and a dedicated research scholar in Psychology. Her journey, marked by a profound dedication to elevating those around her, especially the downtrodden and underprivileged children of society, is a testament to her deep-seated belief in the transformative power of engagement and empathy.

From her earliest days, Minakshi was distinguished by an insatiable appetite for reading. Her literary universe was inhabited by characters and narratives that spanned ethical tales, motivational and inspirational stories, and the mythic parables imbued with life lessons. This voracious reading habit was not merely for personal edification but was driven by a desire to distill and disseminate the essence of these narratives to foster the development of students and peers alike. She was particularly captivated by the lives and teachings of historical figures and spiritual leaders such as Adi Shankaracharya, Swami Vivekananda, Dr. APJ Abdul Kalam, Mahamana Pandit Madan Mohan Malviya, Mahatma Gandhi, Sardar Vallabhai Patel, and Vinoba Bhave, among others. Their philosophies and life stories fueled her ambition to embody their ideals of resilience, selflessness, and relentless pursuit of knowledge.

Dr. Minakshi's academic and practical engagement with psychology has been equally noteworthy. As a research scholar, her focus has been on exploring the intricate tapestry of the human psyche, aiming to unlock the potential for psychological well-being and societal harmony. Her scholarly work is complemented by her active involvement in social work, where she employs her academic insights to make tangible differences in the lives of the underprivileged. Her endeavours in social work are characterized by an innovative approach that combines traditional wisdom with contemporary psychological practices to address the multifaceted challenges faced by these communities.

Her artistic talents, another facet of her diverse capabilities, are not merely a personal passion but also serve as a medium through which she communicates and connects with others. Her art, rich in symbolism and emotional depth, reflects her philosophical inquiries and social concerns, offering viewers a glimpse into the breadth of her intellect and the depth of her compassion.

In addition to her contributions to the arts and social sciences, Dr. Minakshi has embraced the healing arts of Pranic Healing, mastering the techniques developed by Master Choa Kok Sui. This practice, which focuses on the manipulation of Prana or life energy to heal the body and aura, has been both a personal journey of discovery and a means through which she extends her healing touch to others. Her proficiency in Pranic Healing is complemented by her advocacy and teaching of various forms of meditation aimed at rejuvenation, personal betterment, and the cultivation of harmony within individuals and communities alike.

Dr. Minakshi's life is a narrative of relentless pursuit, not just of personal achievement but of the upliftment and empowerment of society at large. Her diverse interests and talents—spanning the arts, literature, psychology, and the healing practices—converge on a singular path of service. She embodies the spirit of the luminaries who inspired her, channelling their legacy through her actions and teachings. Through her books, art, and social initiatives, she continues to inspire a new generation to embark on their own journeys of self-discovery, resilience, and altruism.

Her commitment to social betterment, particularly her focus on uplifting underprivileged children, reflects a deep understanding of the transformative potential of education and personal development. By integrating her knowledge of psychology, her artistic sensibilities, and her healing practices, Dr. Bansal has developed a holistic approach to social work that addresses both the immediate needs and the long-term well-being of the communities she serves.

As an author, Dr. Minakshi's writings offer a blend of inspirational insights, practical wisdom, and reflective contemplations drawn from her extensive reading and life experiences. Her books serve as a guide for those seeking to navigate the complexities of life with grace, resilience, and purpose. Through her narratives, she extends an invitation to her readers to explore the depths of their own potential and to contribute meaningfully to the collective well-being of society.

In Dr. Minakshi Bansal, we find a remarkable synthesis of the artist, the scholar, the healer, and the social activist. Her life's work stands as a beacon of hope and a source of inspiration for individuals seeking to make a difference in the world. Her story is a compelling reminder of the power of individual action, rooted in compassion and driven by a profound commitment to the betterment of humanity. Dr. Minakshi's legacy is not just in the tangible outcomes of her efforts but in the enduring spirit of inquiry, empathy, and service that she embodies.

ppp

Preface

The journey of personal empowerment is both fascinating and complex, weaving together the intricate aspects of psychological concepts with the practicalities of everyday life. It is a path that demands curiosity, introspection, and a commitment to self-improvement that few dare to undertake with sincerity and perseverance. This journey is not just about overcoming the hurdles that life unpredictably throws in our path, but also about understanding the deeper nuances of our thoughts, behaviors, and emotions that dictate our reactions to these challenges.

At the heart of this exploration is the understanding that each individual possesses an innate potential to foster significant changes in their lives. This potential, however, often remains untapped due to various reasons—external pressures, internal fears, and a myriad of social and personal expectations that can cloud our judgment and derail our ambitions. Recognizing and harnessing this potential requires more than just willpower; it requires a profound shift in how we perceive ourselves and our capabilities.

The pursuit of personal empowerment is inherently linked with the concept of self-awareness. To empower oneself truly, one must first understand oneself—acknowledging strengths as proudly as recognizing weaknesses. It is a process that involves peeling back layers of self-deception and confronting sometimes uncomfortable truths. Yet, this process is indispensable because it lays the foundation upon which we can build strategies for personal growth and resilience.

Resilience, a term often tossed around in discussions about mental and emotional health, is far more complex than its usual portrayals. It is not merely about bouncing back from adversity; it's about forging ahead with a greater understanding and a new perspective that emerge from experiencing and overcoming difficulties. It involves developing a mindset that views challenges as catalysts for growth rather than as obstacles. This mindset doesn't develop overnight nor does it arise out of sheer optimism. It is cultivated through consistent efforts—through practices like mindfulness, reflection, and the conscious application of psychological principles in daily life.

One cannot discuss empowerment without touching upon the role of emotions and the necessity of managing them effectively. Emotions can propel us forward or hold us back, and learning to navigate them is crucial in our quest for a balanced and fulfilling life. This is where emotional intelligence plays a pivotal role; it is not just about managing our emotions but also about understanding the emotions of others around us, enhancing our interactions and relationships. It is about using our emotional experiences as stepping stones to deeper insights and more meaningful connections with the world.

Similarly, creativity and self-expression are vital components of personal empowerment. They provide outlets for expressing thoughts and emotions that might be stifled otherwise. Engaging in creative endeavors can be therapeutic; it can also be a means of discovering hidden facets of our personality and of conveying messages that words alone may fail to capture.

However, recognizing and developing these various aspects of our personality and mental framework is only part of the journey. The other, often more challenging part, is integrating these insights into our daily routines. It is about making conscious choices every day that align with our long-term goals and values. It's about setting boundaries that protect our mental and emotional well-being while also pushing ourselves to grow beyond our perceived limits.

Moreover, the process of empowerment is not a solitary journey. It is greatly enriched by interactions with others—learning from their experiences, gaining insights from their perspectives, and supporting each other in our respective paths. Thus, building and nurturing relationships become as much a part of personal development as any self-focused strategy.

This preface sets the stage for a deeper exploration into these themes, inviting readers to reflect on their personal experiences and consider new ways to approach their challenges. It encourages a dialogue with oneself and with the external world, promoting a holistic view of personal development that recognizes the complexity and interconnectedness of various psychological elements.

In essence, this exploration is about equipping oneself with the knowledge and tools to navigate life's complexities with a greater sense of purpose, awareness, and efficacy. It is an invitation to step into a role of greater control and influence over one's own life, to weave through the intricacies of human psychology, and to emerge empowered and enlightened. The journey may be intricate and demanding, but the rewards of such an endeavor are immeasurable and profoundly transformative.

Dr. Minakshi Bansal
Social Activist
Ahmedabad, Gujarat, Bharat

ৡৡৡ

ONE

Introduction to Self-Empowerment

Self-empowerment represents a transformative process where individuals take control and responsibility for their lives by recognizing their intrinsic abilities to effect change. It is an ongoing journey that involves developing confidence, gaining self-awareness, and applying these attributes to meet challenges head-on. The significance of self-empowerment in everyday life cannot be overstated. It equips individuals with the mental tools needed to navigate the complexities of modern existence, from personal challenges to professional obstacles.

Understanding the Concept of Self-Empowerment

Self-empowerment is fundamentally about understanding and utilizing one's own power to initiate changes and make decisions that align with one's goals and values. It involves setting clear objectives, understanding personal strengths and weaknesses, and employing this awareness to guide one's actions and reactions. The empowered individual does not passively await opportunities or external assistance but creates opportunities for themselves.

Empowerment comes from within. It begins with a belief in one's capacity to influence events and outcomes. This belief is not fixed; it grows as one undertakes actions that reinforce their capabilities and as they learn from their experiences. Moreover, self-empowerment is closely tied to self-esteem and self-worth. Individuals who feel empowered believe they deserve success and recognize their right to achieve personal happiness and fulfillment.

The Importance of Self-Empowerment in Everyday Life

The relevance of self-empowerment in daily life extends through every facet of human experience. At its core, it enhances one's ability to make choices that are not dictated by fear, anxiety, or societal pressures but are instead informed by a well-rounded understanding of one's desires and needs.

Decision-Making: Empowered individuals make decisions confidently and independently. This capability is crucial in a world where choices often determine the quality of one's life. By understanding and trusting their judgement, empowered persons navigate through life's decisions more effectively, from the mundane to the significant.

Career and Education: In the realms of work and learning, self-empowerment translates to taking proactive steps towards career advancement and educational development. Empowered people are more likely to pursue opportunities for skill enhancement, negotiate for promotions or raises, and engage in jobs that provide satisfaction and growth.

Relationships: In personal and professional relationships, empowerment means setting boundaries, advocating for oneself, and engaging in healthy, constructive communication. Empowered individuals are better equipped to form and maintain relationships that are reciprocal and respectful.

Mental Health: Self-empowerment also has profound implications for mental health. By fostering a sense of control and self-efficacy, empowerment can act as a buffer against stress, anxiety, and depression. Feeling empowered helps individuals manage their emotions effectively and approach life's stresses with resilience.

Cultivating Self-Empowerment

Developing self-empowerment involves several key steps, starting with self-reflection. Individuals must take the time to understand their values, passions, and goals. This understanding lays the groundwork for setting meaningful personal and professional objectives. The next step involves expanding one's knowledge and skills, which not only increases competence but also boosts confidence in one's ability to handle new challenges.

It is also essential to cultivate a positive mindset that focuses on growth and potential rather than limitations. Such a mindset embraces challenges as opportunities for learning rather than obstacles. Furthermore, building a supportive network can enhance one's empowerment. Being surrounded by individuals who encourage and believe in one's abilities can reinforce one's self-belief and motivate one to persist despite setbacks.

Self-empowerment is crucial for leading a fulfilling life. It allows individuals to live authentically and effectively, making decisions that align with their deepest values and aspirations. By embracing the principles of empowerment, individuals not only enhance their own lives but also contribute positively to their communities and societies. As we continue to understand and apply this empowering framework, the potential for personal and collective progress is limitless.

ppp

"Empowerment is about more than just taking control; it's about discovering and nurturing your own innate abilities to influence the world around you. Recognize your strengths, embrace your weaknesses, and continue to grow towards your full potential."

ᕘᕘᕘ

TWO
THE PSYCHOLOGY OF SELF-MOTIVATION

Self-motivation is an essential component of empowerment. It is the internal drive that propels individuals to initiate and continue actions towards achieving personal goals without external compulsion or significant reward. Understanding the psychology behind self-motivation is crucial for anyone seeking to harness this powerful force to achieve success and personal fulfillment.

Exploring the Drivers Behind Our Motivations

Motivation can be broadly categorized into two types: intrinsic and extrinsic. Intrinsic motivation arises from within the individual—it is the motivation to engage in a behavior because it is personally rewarding. Essentially, performing the activity is its own reward. Activities like reading a book because you enjoy the story or working out because you relish the feeling of vitality are driven by intrinsic motivation.

Extrinsic motivation, on the other hand, involves performing actions to earn a reward or avoid punishment. This could include studying hard to get good grades or working late to earn a bonus. Understanding these two types of motivations is key to harnessing the full power of self-motivation.

Intrinsic Motivation: The Heart of Self-Motivation

Intrinsic motivation is often more powerful and enduring than extrinsic motivation because it taps into the core values and interests of the individual. When people are intrinsically motivated, they are more likely to pursue activities with energy and persistence. This is because the activities align with what they find meaningful and interesting, making the process enjoyable and the challenges worthwhile.

Several psychological theories help explain how intrinsic motivation works. One of the most influential theories is the Self-Determination Theory (SDT), which posits that intrinsic motivation is enhanced when three basic psychological needs are satisfied: autonomy, competence, and relatedness. Autonomy refers to feeling in control of one's actions and choices; competence involves feeling skilled and capable of meeting challenges; and relatedness refers to feeling connected to others.

By satisfying these three needs, activities not only become more enjoyable but also more meaningful. For instance, a writer who chooses to work on a novel independently (autonomy), gradually improves their writing skills through practice (competence), and shares their work with a supportive community (relatedness), is likely to be highly motivated to keep writing.

Harnessing Intrinsic Motivation

To harness intrinsic motivation, it is essential to engage in self-reflection to understand what one truly values and enjoys. This could involve identifying hobbies that ignite passion or professional tasks that are especially fulfilling. Once these are identified, setting personal goals that align with these interests can significantly boost motivation.

Creating environments that foster autonomy is also crucial. This might involve tailoring tasks so they provide adequate freedom and control, or choosing projects that allow for creativity and personal input. Additionally, seeking out challenges that are at the right level of difficulty can enhance competence without leading to frustration or disengagement.

The Role of Extrinsic Motivation

While intrinsic motivation is ideal for long-term satisfaction and persistence, extrinsic motivation plays an important role in driving behavior, especially in activities that individuals may not inherently enjoy. Recognizing when to leverage extrinsic rewards can be effective, especially in initiating an activity that one might not choose to do otherwise.

For extrinsic motivation to be effective without undermining intrinsic motivation, it should be used judiciously. Rewards should be seen as acknowledgments of effort rather than bribes, and they should not be the sole reason for undertaking a task. Over time, extrinsically motivated activities can often lead to the development of intrinsic motivation, especially as individuals find aspects of the task they can enjoy or take pride in.

Balancing Motivation for Optimal Performance

The most effective approach to self-motivation involves balancing intrinsic and extrinsic motivations. By understanding and managing both types of motivations, individuals can optimize their motivation across different settings and tasks. For instance, a student might study for exams out of a desire for good grades (extrinsic motivation) while also finding joy in learning new things about subjects they love (intrinsic motivation).

Self-motivation is a complex yet vital force that drives personal achievement and satisfaction. By understanding the psychological underpinnings of motivational drives and learning how to harness them, individuals can empower themselves to pursue their goals with enthusiasm and resilience. The journey towards mastering self-motivation not only enhances personal success but also contributes to a richer, more fulfilling life.

ᐅᐅᐅ

"Resilience isn't just recovering from the hard knocks of life; it's using each setback as a stepping stone to a stronger, wiser self. It's about finding the courage within to face each challenge with a smile."

ᚦᚦᚦ

THREE

RECOGNIZING AND OVERCOMING FEAR

Fear is a fundamental human emotion that is both complex and powerful. It can protect us from danger, but it can also hinder our ability to grow and achieve our full potential. Recognizing and overcoming fear is therefore a crucial step in the process of self-empowerment and personal development.

Understanding the Nature of Fear

Fear manifests in many ways, from physical dangers to psychological and existential threats. It can be acute, as in the fear felt during a dangerous situation, or it can be chronic, such as the ongoing anxiety about failing to meet personal or professional expectations. Regardless of its form, the impact of fear on an individual's life can be profound. It can limit one's ability to take risks, try new things, and pursue opportunities.

To begin addressing fear, it is essential to understand its origins and triggers. This understanding starts with self-awareness—being mindful of the situations, thoughts, or environments that provoke fear. For many, this might involve fears related to social rejection, financial insecurity, or personal inadequacy. By identifying these triggers, individuals can begin to devise strategies to confront and manage their fears effectively.

Identifying Fears

Identifying one's fears requires honest self-reflection. This process can be facilitated through journaling, meditation, or therapy, which can help individuals explore their inner thoughts and feelings. Recognizing specific fears is the first step towards confronting them, rather than avoiding or suppressing them.

Once fears are identified, it's helpful to categorize them based on their nature and impact. Some fears might be based on realistic assessments of danger, while others might be exaggerated or irrational. Distinguishing between these can help individuals focus on what is genuinely threatening and dismiss fears that are unfounded or overly speculative.

Strategies to Overcome Fear

Overcoming fear is not about eliminating it entirely but rather learning how to manage it effectively. Several strategies can be employed to help individuals cope with and ultimately reduce the impact of their fears.

Exposure Therapy: One of the most effective ways to reduce fear is through gradual and repeated exposure to the fear source itself. This technique, often used in cognitive-behavioral therapy, involves facing the fear in a controlled and safe environment, gradually increasing the exposure intensity as the individual becomes less sensitive to the trigger.

Cognitive Restructuring: This technique involves identifying and challenging the negative thoughts that contribute to fear. By questioning the validity of these thoughts and replacing them with more balanced and constructive ones, individuals can reduce the intensity of their fears.

Mindfulness and Relaxation Techniques: Practices such as meditation, deep breathing, and progressive muscle relaxation can help calm the mind and body, reducing the physiological and emotional intensity of fear. These techniques are particularly useful for managing anxiety and stress-related fears.

Building Resilience and Self-Efficacy: Increasing one's confidence in handling challenges can diminish fear. This can be achieved through skill development, achieving small goals, and recalling past successes. As individuals build their competence and resilience, their fear of unknown or challenging situations decreases.

Seeking Support: Sometimes, the best way to overcome fear is by seeking support from others. This could be professional help, such as therapy, or support from peers, such as support groups or friends and family who understand and encourage facing fears.

Personal Growth Through Overcoming Fear

Overcoming fear is inherently linked to personal growth. As individuals confront and manage their fears, they open themselves up to new experiences and opportunities for learning and development. The process of overcoming fear is transformative; it not only reduces the negative impact of fear but also builds a set of skills and attributes that contribute to a more empowered and fulfilling life.

Recognizing and overcoming fear is a dynamic and challenging journey that requires courage, self-awareness, and persistent effort. The strategies outlined here provide a framework for addressing fears constructively and effectively. By embracing these approaches, individuals can move beyond their fears, unlock their potential, and achieve a greater sense of freedom and achievement in their lives.

ৡৡৡ

"Positive thinking does not ignore life's challenges,
instead, it reframes them into opportunities for
growth. Choose optimism, for with it, every obstacle
becomes a teacher and every hardship a possibility
for progress."

▷▷▷

FOUR

BUILDING RESILIENCE

Resilience is the capacity to recover quickly from difficulties; it's what enables people to emerge from challenging experiences with a positive outlook and renewed strength. This essential quality can be developed and refined through specific strategies, transforming how we handle life's adversities.

Understanding Resilience

Resilience is not an innate trait that people either have or do not have; it involves behaviors, thoughts, and actions that can be learned and developed by anyone. A resilient individual doesn't avoid difficulties but faces them head-on, learning and growing from these experiences. This ability to adapt and thrive in the face of challenges is crucial for personal and professional success.

The core of resilience lies in our ability to manage our thoughts and actions. It is fostered through a positive, realistic outlook and a belief that we can influence our outcomes. With resilience, individuals maintain their calm and look for ways to resolve problems, viewing setbacks as temporary and surmountable.

Techniques for Developing Resilience

Developing resilience is a multi-faceted process that involves strengthening various personal capabilities. The following techniques are central to cultivating resilience:

Maintaining a Positive Outlook: Keeping a positive attitude is not about ignoring the reality of a situation but about maintaining a hopeful outlook. It's about seeing life's challenges as opportunities for growth. A positive outlook helps to mitigate feelings of helplessness and despair and fosters a sense of well-being and control.

Emotional Awareness and Regulation: Understanding and managing your emotions is crucial in building resilience. People who can identify what they're feeling and why they're feeling it can decide how to act on those feelings more effectively. Techniques such as mindfulness, meditation, and cognitive-behavioral strategies can help individuals manage their emotional responses to stress.

Strengthening Connections: Building strong, positive relationships with loved ones and peers can provide the emotional support needed to weather tough times. Having a support network can give access to advice, guidance, and encouragement, which are invaluable during times of crisis.

Problem-Solving Skills: Being able to look at a problem and identify a solution is crucial for resilience. This not only involves analytical thinking but also creativity and flexibility. The ability to step back from a problem, view it from multiple angles, and approach it without panic is essential.

Self-Care: Taking care of one's health—physical, mental, and emotional—is foundational to resilience. Regular physical activity, adequate sleep, and proper nutrition help maintain high levels of energy and focus. Self-care also involves engaging in hobbies and activities that you enjoy, which can distract from stress and replenish your energy.

Goal Setting and Achievement: Setting and working towards goals provides a sense of purpose and direction. Resilient individuals use setbacks as learning opportunities that can inform their future strategies. Achieving small goals can also build confidence, which in turn boosts resilience.

Learning from Experience: Resilience can be developed by reflecting on past experiences and drawing lessons from them, whether they are successes or failures. This reflection can enhance understanding and promote better decision-making in the future.

Flexibility: Life often involves adjusting our paths when initial plans don't work out. Resilient people are flexible in adjusting their goals and finding new ways to move forward when faced with challenges.

Applying Resilience in Daily Life

Applying these resilience-building techniques in everyday life requires conscious effort and practice. It might start with changing how one responds to small, daily stressors to build up the skills and confidence to handle bigger challenges. Over time, these practices can become second nature, greatly enhancing an individual's ability to deal with whatever adversities they might face.

Resilience is a powerful tool that enables individuals to navigate the complexities of life with strength and grace. By actively developing resilience through the techniques discussed, individuals can enhance their ability to adapt, overcome adversities, and lead fulfilling lives. As resilience grows, so does the capacity for personal growth and achievement, paving the way for a confident, productive, and positive life.

ᙏᙏᙏ

"Emotional intelligence is the silent language of the heart that strengthens connections and builds worlds of understanding. Listen closely, empathize deeply, and act compassionately."

❦❦❦

FIVE

The Power of Positive Thinking

Positive thinking is more than just a tagline. It changes the way we behave, and its impact on our lives is profound. Having a positive mindset allows individuals to approach life's challenges with a more optimistic and productive outlook, shaping their realities and significantly influencing their success.

How Positive Thoughts Shape Our Reality

The concept of positive thinking refers to the process of nurturing thoughts that create energy, hope, and a belief in good outcomes. The way we think about ourselves and our lives has a direct influence on our reality. Positive thinking fosters a range of beneficial traits including resilience, mental health, motivation, and persistence in the face of challenges.

One of the primary ways in which positive thoughts shape our reality is through the lens of cognitive bias. Cognitive biases are systematic patterns of deviation from norm or rationality in judgment, whereby inferences about other people and situations may be drawn in an illogical fashion.

People who engage in positive thinking are more likely to experience a beneficial bias called the "optimism bias," which prompts individuals to expect good outcomes.

Influence of Positive Thinking on Success

The influence of positive thoughts on success is evident across various aspects of life. In the realm of personal growth, individuals who maintain a positive outlook are more likely to pursue goals and opportunities, face setbacks with tenacity, and maintain a higher level of self-esteem and overall well-being.

Enhanced Resilience: Positive thinkers are better equipped to handle stress and adversity. Their positive outlook enables them to see difficult situations as opportunities for growth rather than insurmountable problems. They are less likely to succumb to the stress and are more likely to recover quickly from setbacks due to their optimistic mindset.

Improved Health: Research has shown that positive thinking can lead to a range of health benefits, including longer life span, lower rates of depression, lower levels of distress, greater resistance to the common cold, better psychological and physical well-being, and better cardiovascular health and reduced risk of death from cardiovascular disease.

Stronger Relationships: Positive thinkers are more likely to foster supportive relationships. Their positive attitude towards life can be infectious, helping them to maintain healthier interactions and a wider social network, which in turn can provide increased support during tough times.

Greater Achievement: Positive thoughts can increase one's motivation and energy levels, enhancing commitment to goals. Individuals who are optimistic are also more persistent, which is often required to achieve high levels of success.

Techniques to Cultivate Positive Thinking

While the benefits of positive thinking are extensive, maintaining an optimistic outlook requires practice and dedication. Below are techniques to cultivate and maintain a positive mindset:

Affirmations and Positive Self-Talk: Affirmations are positive statements that can help you to challenge and overcome self-sabotaging and negative thoughts. When you repeatedly practice positive affirmations, you can start to make significant changes to your self-esteem, confidence, and motivation.

Mindfulness and Meditation: These practices help individuals focus on the present moment and become more aware of their thoughts and feelings.

Mindfulness encourages a heightened state of awareness and acceptance of the present, which can mitigate the impact of negative thoughts.

Gratitude: Keeping a gratitude journal, where you reflect on the day's positive events, can shift your focus away from negativity and toward what is positive in your life. This practice can alter the way you perceive situations and foster a more optimistic outlook.

Visualize Success: Visualization is a technique where you picture yourself achieving your goals. It is a powerful way to build your confidence and reduce the fear associated with failure.

The power of positive thinking is transformative. It shapes our perceptions, influences our physical and mental health, affects our relationships, and plays a significant role in our overall success.

By consciously practicing and cultivating positive thinking, individuals can enhance their resilience and approach life's challenges with a proactive and optimistic mindset, thereby increasing their chances for success and a fulfilling life.

❧❧❧

"Setting goals is the first step in turning the
invisible into the visible. Define your dreams, break
them into achievable steps, and watch your visions
transform into reality."

SIX

CULTIVATING EMOTIONAL INTELLIGENCE

Emotional intelligence (EI) is the ability to recognize, understand, and manage our own emotions and to recognize, understand, and influence the emotions of others. Cultivating emotional intelligence is crucial for both personal and professional success, as it enhances communication, improves relationships, and promotes emotional health and well-being.

Understanding Emotional Intelligence

The concept of emotional intelligence encompasses several key skills: self-awareness, self-regulation, motivation, empathy, and social skills. These skills enable individuals to navigate social complexities with more awareness and effectiveness, and to make personal decisions that achieve positive results.

Self-awareness involves recognizing one's emotions and their impact on thoughts and behavior. It includes accurate self-assessment and self-confidence.

Self-regulation refers to managing one's emotions healthily and constructively, maintaining control and adaptability in various situations.

Motivation covers the drive to pursue goals with energy and persistence.

Empathy is the ability to understand the emotional makeup of other people.

Social skills involve managing relationships to move people in desired directions, whether in leading, negotiating, or working as part of a team.

Improving Awareness and Management of Your Emotions

Cultivating emotional intelligence starts with improving self-awareness. You can enhance your self-awareness by keeping an emotions diary, which helps to track what triggers your emotions and how you respond to them. This reflection can provide insights into your emotional patterns and offer clues on how to better manage them.

Once you become more aware of your emotions, you can work on self-regulation. Techniques such as mindfulness, deep breathing, and meditation can help you maintain control over your emotions and prevent them from overwhelming you. This control allows you to think before reacting and to manage your emotional responses more effectively.

Enhancing the Awareness and Management of Others' Emotions

Empathy is a critical aspect of emotional intelligence that involves not only understanding others' emotions but also responding to them appropriately. Developing empathy requires active listening and paying attention to non-verbal cues such as body language, facial expressions, and tone of voice. By truly listening to others, you can better understand their emotions and respond in ways that are considerate of their feelings.

Social skills are also vital. These are the skills used to communicate effectively, manage conflicts, lead teams, and build lasting relationships. Enhancing these skills involves learning how to communicate clearly and effectively, how to listen actively, and how to resolve conflicts constructively.

Techniques for Developing Emotional Intelligence

Mindfulness and Self-Reflection: Practicing mindfulness and engaging in regular self-reflection can help you become more aware of your emotions and how they affect your thoughts and actions. This awareness is the first step in managing your emotions effectively.

Emotional Regulation Techniques: Learning techniques to manage stress and emotional upheaval can help you maintain your emotional balance. Practices like guided imagery, relaxation techniques, and structured problem-solving can all contribute to better emotional regulation.

Feedback and Social Awareness: Regular feedback from friends, family, or colleagues can provide valuable insights into how you are perceived by others, which can help in adjusting your behaviors and improving your social interactions.

Empathy Exercises: Putting yourself in someone else's shoes or trying to think from their perspective can enhance your empathy. This could be as simple as asking questions about their experiences and feelings, and genuinely considering their responses.

Social Skills Practice: Engaging in group activities, whether professional or recreational, can improve your social skills. These activities provide opportunities to practice communication, conflict resolution, and teamwork.

Cultivating emotional intelligence is a powerful process that enhances how we connect with others and ourselves. It improves our ability to manage our emotions, understand others' emotions, and navigate social interactions more effectively. By developing emotional intelligence, we not only enhance our personal relationships but also increase our professional effectiveness, making it an invaluable skill set for personal growth and career success.

ϷϷϷ

"Creativity is the soul's palette; it colors our
experiences, shapes our identity, and paints the
canvas of our lives. Dive into your imagination,
express your deepest emotions, and let your unique
colors shine."

SEVEN

SETTING AND ACHIEVING GOALS

Setting and achieving goals is a fundamental part of personal and professional development. Goals provide direction, help measure progress, and motivate individuals to push through obstacles and challenges. Understanding how to set realistic goals and effectively strategize to achieve them is crucial for success.

The Importance of Goal Setting

Goals serve as a roadmap, guiding actions and ensuring that efforts are focused on achieving meaningful results. They help maintain motivation over the long term by setting a defined target to strive towards. Additionally, goals allow for the tracking of progress, which can be incredibly motivating and can help refine strategies as needed.

Effective Methods for Setting Realistic Goals

SMART Goals: The SMART criteria is one of the most effective frameworks for setting goals. Goals should be Specific, Measurable, Achievable, Relevant, and Time-bound. This framework ensures that goals are well-defined and within reach, making it easier to plan actions and measure progress.

Align Goals with Values: Goals that are aligned with personal or professional values are more motivating and easier to commit to. When goals reflect what is truly important to an individual, they carry a deeper sense of purpose and fulfillment.

Break Goals into Manageable Steps: Large goals can seem daunting and unachievable. Breaking them down into smaller, manageable tasks can make them more approachable and less overwhelming. This step-by-step approach also helps maintain momentum and motivation as each smaller goal is achieved.

Write Down Goals: Writing goals down not only helps clarify what you want to achieve but also serves as a visual reminder of what you are working towards. Written goals are easier to review regularly, keeping them at the forefront of your mind.

Strategies to Achieve Goals

Once goals are set, the focus shifts to achieving them. This requires a combination of motivation, planning, and ongoing evaluation.

Develop an Action Plan: Every goal needs a clear action plan detailing the steps necessary to achieve it. This plan should include timelines, resources needed, and potential obstacles. A detailed plan helps anticipate challenges and prepares you to face them effectively.

Use Time Management Tools: Effective time management is crucial for achieving goals. Utilizing tools such as calendars, planners, and apps can help schedule time for necessary actions and track progress. Time management also involves prioritizing tasks based on their importance and urgency.

Monitor and Adjust Your Progress: Regularly check your progress towards your goals. This monitoring can help you stay on track and motivate you to continue. If progress is slower than expected, don't hesitate to adjust your strategies or timelines. Flexibility is key in successfully achieving goals.

Seek Feedback: Feedback from others can provide new insights and help refine your approach. Whether it's from a mentor, coach, or peers, constructive feedback is invaluable for improvement and development.

Maintain Motivation: Keeping motivation high can be challenging, especially for long-term goals. Find ways to keep yourself motivated, whether through rewards for achieving milestones, maintaining a positive mindset, or surrounding yourself with supportive people.

Visualize Success: Regular visualization of achieving your goals can be a powerful motivator. It helps reinforce the belief in the possibility of success and clarifies the benefits of reaching your goals.

Applying Goal-Setting in Daily Life

Incorporating goal-setting into daily life can transform how you approach both personal and professional challenges. It provides a structured way to organize efforts, making even the most ambitious objectives attainable. By continually setting and achieving goals, you can systematically enhance various aspects of your life, leading to increased satisfaction and success.

Setting and achieving goals is a dynamic process that requires careful planning, dedication, and periodic reassessment. The ability to effectively set and pursue goals not only leads to achievement but also contributes to a greater sense of purpose and fulfillment. Adopting these methods and strategies can help anyone achieve their aspirations and continuously grow and improve in all areas of life.

❧❧❧

"Mindfulness is the quiet victory over chaos and clutter. By being present in the moment, you command your life to unfold at your feet, rich with detail and vibrantly alive."

❦❦❦

EIGHT

THE ROLE OF RELATIONSHIPS IN PERSONAL GROWTH

Relationships play a crucial role in personal development. They act as mirrors reflecting our true selves back to us, providing feedback, support, and the challenge needed to grow. Understanding the impact of relationships on personal growth and learning to cultivate supportive connections can greatly enhance an individual's ability to develop and thrive.

Understanding the Impact of Relationships on Personal Development

Relationships affect personal growth in several profound ways. They provide emotional support, challenge us to transcend our limitations, and influence our motivations and behaviors. The quality and depth of our relationships can either propel us forward on our journey of self-improvement or hold us back.

Emotional Support: Supportive relationships provide a safety net of emotional comfort that can help individuals cope with stress and adversity. Knowing that there is someone who believes in you and backs you up can boost your confidence and willingness to take risks or try new things, which are essential for personal growth.

Feedback and Reflection: Relationships also serve as a source of feedback. Friends, family members, colleagues, and mentors can offer insights into our behavior and attitudes that we may not see ourselves. This feedback is crucial for self-awareness, one of the cornerstones of personal development.

Challenge and Encouragement: Sometimes, relationships push us out of our comfort zones. Be it through challenge or encouragement, these interactions compel us to grow and improve. Relationships that challenge us can lead to significant personal growth by forcing us to confront our fears, change our habits, and adopt new perspectives.

Role Models: Relationships with individuals who embody traits we admire can inspire us to adopt similar behaviors and attitudes. Role models play an integral part in shaping our aspirations and behaviors through their example.

Shared Experiences and Learning: Through relationships, we gain access to new experiences and information. Each interaction with another person can teach us something new about the world, about others, and about ourselves.

Cultivating Supportive Connections

Developing supportive relationships is a deliberate process that involves recognizing the qualities that contribute to personal growth and nurturing those connections.

Choose Relationships Wisely: It's important to invest time and energy into relationships that are nurturing and positive. Look for people who are supportive, positive, and understanding—those who encourage you to be your best self.

Communicate Openly and Honestly: Effective communication is the foundation of any good relationship. Being able to express your thoughts and feelings openly and to listen sincerely to others are key for deepening connections.

Be Supportive: To cultivate supportive relationships, you must also be supportive. This means being there for others during their times of need, offering encouragement, and celebrating their successes as if they were your own.

Set Boundaries: Healthy relationships require boundaries. Setting and respecting boundaries with others ensures that relationships are mutually respectful and supportive.

Nurture Empathy and Understanding: Try to see things from the other person's perspective. Empathy fosters deeper understanding and connection, which are crucial for supportive relationships.

Engage in Shared Activities: Shared interests and activities can strengthen relationships. They provide opportunities to connect in meaningful ways and can lead to shared growth and learning.

Seek Diversity in Relationships: Diverse relationships expose us to different perspectives and ideas, enhancing our personal growth. They challenge our worldviews and encourage us to think in new ways.

Applying Relationship Insights to Personal Growth

Integrating the insights gained from relationships into personal growth involves reflection and action. Reflect on the feedback and experiences you receive from your relationships and consider how they apply to your personal development goals. Use this information to adjust your behaviors, enhance your strengths, improve your weaknesses, and make more informed decisions about your life.

Relationships are fundamental to personal growth. They challenge us, support us, provide us with new perspectives, and mirror our progress. By understanding the role relationships play in our development and actively working to cultivate supportive connections, we can significantly enhance our journey towards personal growth and fulfillment. These connections not only enrich our lives but also propel us towards becoming more well-rounded and effective individuals.

ᑭᑭᑭ

"Change is the law of life, and those who look only to the past or present are certain to miss the future. Embrace change, for it is the universe's invitation to grow and learn."

ᐅᐅᐅ

NINE

MINDFULNESS AND PRESENCE

In today's fast-paced world, staying present and mindful can seem like a challenging task. Distractions are everywhere, pulling our attention in multiple directions. However, developing mindfulness and enhancing our ability to stay present can profoundly impact our quality of life, improving our focus, reducing stress, and fostering a deeper understanding of ourselves and our surroundings.

Understanding Mindfulness and Presence

Mindfulness is the practice of being fully aware and present in the moment without judgment. It involves a conscious direction of our awareness. We are present when we are fully engaged in what we are doing, not overpowered by distractions or dwelling in thoughts of the past or future.

Presence is similar but focuses more on the quality of being in the moment with others or in a particular situation. It's about how we engage and connect in the moments of life. Both mindfulness and presence can be developed through practice and can lead to more satisfying and productive experiences.

Techniques for Enhancing Mindfulness and Presence

Meditation: Meditation is one of the most effective tools for developing mindfulness. It trains the brain to focus on the present and reduces the tendency to ruminate on the past or worry about the future.

There are many types of meditation, including focused attention, where you concentrate on a single point of reference such as your breath; and open monitoring meditation, where you observe all aspects of your experience, without attachment.

Mindful Breathing: This involves focusing your attention on your breath, the inhale and exhale. You can do this while sitting or lying down in a quiet place, just a few minutes each day can significantly increase your ability to be mindful and present.

Body Scans: Another meditation technique, body scanning, involves paying attention to parts of the body and bodily sensations in a gradual sequence from feet to head. This practice encourages you to inhabit your body more fully and promotes physical and mental relaxation.

Mindful Observation: This practice involves picking a natural object within your immediate environment and focusing on watching it for a minute or two.

This could be a flower, an insect, or the clouds moving across the sky. The key is to watch it as if you are seeing it for the first time, viscerally exploring every aspect of its formation, color, texture, and function.

Mindful Listening: This technique involves listening to sounds in your environment with a non-judgmental presence. This could be the chirping of birds, the hum of a refrigerator, or even the sounds of traffic. Listen to the loud and the subtle without attaching any personal significance to them.

Mindful Eating: This involves paying full attention to the experience of eating and drinking, both inside and outside the body. Notice the color, texture, and flavor of the food, savor each part, and listen to your body when hunger arises and when it feels satiated.

Gratitude Practice: Taking time each day to think about things you are grateful for encourages a positive focus and helps you appreciate the moment. This can be done through writing a gratitude journal or simply taking a few moments to mentally acknowledge these things.

Digital Detox: Set aside time to disconnect from digital devices to overcome the brain's habituation to constant stimulation. This helps in reducing anxiety and increasing attention span.

Single-Tasking: Instead of multi-tasking, focus on one task at a time. This leads to improved efficiency and less mental clutter. Single-tasking ensures that you are fully present and engaged in the task at hand, which enhances performance.

Integrating Mindfulness into Everyday Life

The key to integrating mindfulness into your life is to make it a part of your daily routine. It doesn't need to take a lot of time or effort; even a few minutes a day can make a significant difference. Regular practice can help these techniques become automatic responses that enhance your ability to stay present and reduce stress in your life.

The practice of mindfulness and staying present offers a reprieve from the hectic pace of modern life. It fosters a greater appreciation for the moment, improves mental and physical health, and enhances overall well-being.

By regularly practicing mindfulness techniques, we can develop better control over our responses to life's challenges and lead more focused, productive, and fulfilling lives.

ᚦᚦᚦ

"Happiness is not a station you arrive at, but a manner of traveling. Make each journey joyful by appreciating the here and now, and finding contentment in the everyday."

ᗞᗞᗞ

TEN

COPING WITH STRESS

Stress is an inevitable part of life. Whether it comes from daily responsibilities, sudden changes, or long-term challenges, its effects can impact our mental and physical health. Learning how to effectively cope with stress is crucial for maintaining overall well-being and for leading a productive and fulfilling life.

Understanding Stress and Its Effects

Stress is the body's response to any demand for change. This response can be physical, mental, or emotional and is triggered by both positive and negative experiences. In small doses, stress can be beneficial, providing the motivation and energy to face challenges. However, chronic stress can lead to serious health problems, including mental health disorders, cardiovascular disease, and a weakened immune system.

Practical Tips for Managing Stress

To manage stress effectively, it's important to develop a comprehensive approach that includes lifestyle changes, coping techniques, and sometimes professional help. Here are several practical strategies for managing stress:

Identify Stressors: The first step in managing stress is to identify what causes it. Keeping a stress journal can help track the situations that create stress. Note how you respond to the stress, both emotionally and physically, and what you did to make yourself feel better.

Develop Healthy Responses: Instead of coping with stress in unhealthy ways such as overeating or undereating, smoking, or using drugs or alcohol, try to develop healthy ways to cope. Exercise regularly, engage in hobbies you enjoy, practice relaxation techniques, and spend time with loved ones.

Establish Boundaries: In today's digital world, it's easy to feel pressure to be available 24 hours a day. Establish some work-life boundaries for yourself. That might mean making a rule not to check email from home in the evening, or not answering the phone during dinner time.

Take Time to Recharge: To avoid the negative effects of chronic stress and burnout, we need time to replenish and return to our pre-stress level of functioning. This recovery process requires "switching off" from work by having periods of time when you are neither engaging in work-related activities, nor thinking about work. That's why it's crucial to disconnect from time to time, in a way that fits your needs and preferences.

Learn to Relax: Techniques such as meditation, deep breathing exercises, and mindfulness (a practice that involves staying fully present and engaged in the moment) can help melt away stress. Start by taking a few minutes each day to focus on a simple activity like breathing, walking, or enjoying a meal. The skill of being able to focus purposefully on a single activity without distraction will get stronger with practice and you'll find that you can apply it to many different aspects of your life.

Talk About Your Problems: If something is bothering you, talking about it can help lower your stress. You can talk to family members, friends, a trusted clergyman, your doctor, or a therapist.

Maintain a Positive Attitude: Try to practice positive self-talk every day — doing things like thinking, "I can do this," "I'm doing my best," or "I can handle this if I take one step at a time." By doing these things, you can reduce stress by focusing on positive outcomes rather than negative fears.

Get Enough Sleep: Sleep affects your mood and your body's ability to handle stress. Ensure you get around seven to eight hours of quality sleep each night to help manage stress levels.

Manage Your Time: Poor time management can cause a lot of stress. When you're stretched too thin and running behind, it's hard to stay calm and focused. Plus, you'll be tempted to avoid or cut back on all the healthy things you should be doing to reduce stress, like socializing and getting enough sleep. The good news: there are things you can do to achieve a healthier work-life balance.

Integrating Stress Management Techniques into Daily Life

Successfully managing stress is not about completely eliminating it but about learning how to control how much it affects you. Integrating stress management techniques into daily life requires consistency and commitment. With regular practice, these techniques can fundamentally change your brain's response to stress.

Effectively coping with stress involves taking proactive steps to reduce stressors, adopting healthy ways to manage stress, and being prepared to take care of yourself when faced with stressful situations. By integrating these practices into your daily life, you can improve your resilience and enhance your overall well-being.

❦❦❦

"Bad habits are chains that are too light to feel until they are too heavy to carry. Identify them early, understand their triggers, and replace them with actions that uplift and fulfill."

ᛈᛈᛈ

ELEVEN

HARNESSING PERSONAL STRENGTHS

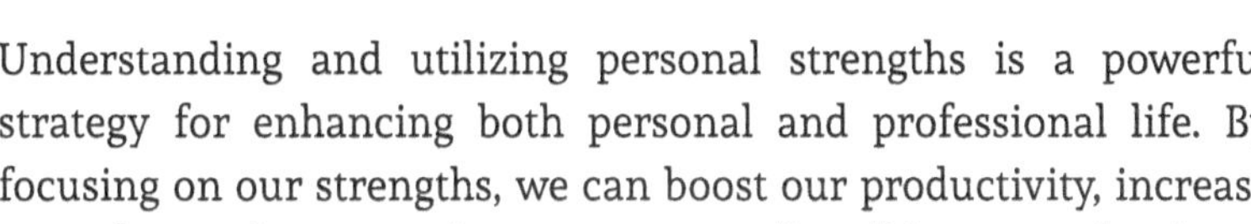

Understanding and utilizing personal strengths is a powerful strategy for enhancing both personal and professional life. By focusing on our strengths, we can boost our productivity, increase our job satisfaction, enhance our overall well-being, and achieve more in our careers.

Identifying Personal Strengths

The first step in harnessing your strengths is identifying them. This involves more than just acknowledging what you are good at; it also includes recognizing your values, where you excel, and the activities that energize you.

Self-Assessment: Start by reflecting on past experiences where you felt particularly proud or successful. What tasks were you performing? What skills did you use? Tools such as the StrengthsFinder assessment or the VIA Character Strengths survey can provide a structured approach to discovering your strengths.

Feedback Analysis: Another effective way to identify your strengths is through feedback from others. This can come from performance reviews, 360-degree feedback, or simply asking colleagues, friends, and family what they see as your strengths. People often observe capabilities that you may not recognize in yourself.

Experimentation: Engage in new activities and pay attention to how you perform and feel. Experimenting with different tasks can reveal hidden strengths and help clarify which skills and activities you are naturally drawn to and excel in.

Utilizing Your Strengths

Once you have a clear understanding of your strengths, the next step is to put them to use in enhancing your life.

Career Advancement: Tailor your career path to align more closely with your strengths. People who use their strengths every day are more likely to be engaged and excel in their work. Seek roles that allow you to play to your strengths, or speak with your manager about adjusting your current role to better suit your abilities.

Goal Setting: Set personal and professional goals based on your strengths. This alignment increases your likelihood of success and satisfaction as it allows you to work in ways that naturally suit you.

Skill Development: While it's important to address weaknesses, investing in your strengths will often yield more significant returns. Develop your strengths through further training and practice, and find new ways to apply them in different aspects of your life.

Team Contribution: Understand how your strengths complement those of others in your team. By recognizing how your strengths fit into the broader team context, you can better position yourself as a key contributor and collaborator.

Problem Solving: Leverage your strengths in problem-solving situations. Whether in personal challenges or professional projects, applying your strengths can lead to more innovative and effective solutions.

Building Relationships: Use your strengths to build and deepen relationships. For example, if one of your strengths is empathy, you might use that ability to connect with and understand the needs of your colleagues or friends better.

Balancing Strengths and Weaknesses

While focusing on strengths is important, it's also necessary to be aware of and manage weaknesses. The goal is not to ignore weaknesses but to prevent them from undermining your strengths. Strategies for managing weaknesses include:

Developing Skills: For weaknesses that can be improved and are critical for your success, consider targeted development efforts.

Strategic Partnerships: Pair up with others who have complementary strengths to cover areas of weakness.

Outsourcing: In some cases, it may be more efficient to outsource tasks that fall into your weaker areas.

Redesigning Tasks: Modify how you perform tasks to better play to your strengths.

Integrating Strengths into Daily Life

Integrating your strengths into your daily life can enhance your effectiveness and satisfaction. It requires conscious effort and ongoing adjustment. Regular reflection and feedback are key to ensuring that you continue to focus on your strengths and align your activities with them.

Effectively harnessing personal strengths involves identifying what you are good at, actively seeking opportunities to use those strengths, and strategically managing weaknesses. By focusing on your strengths, you not only improve your own performance and satisfaction but also enhance your contributions to your team and community. This strengths-based approach can lead to more fulfilling and successful personal and professional lives.

ᑭᑭᑭ

"To integrate psychological wisdom into your life is to weave a richer tapestry of understanding, not just of oneself but of all human interaction. Everyday brings a new lesson; be eager to learn."

ԁԁԁ

TWELVE
Overcoming Procrastination

Procrastination, the act of delaying or postponing tasks, is a common behavior that can hinder personal and professional progress. Understanding why we procrastinate and developing strategies to combat it can significantly enhance productivity and reduce stress.

Understanding Why We Procrastinate

Procrastination is not simply a matter of poor time management or laziness but often involves deeper psychological reasons. Here are some common causes:

Fear of Failure: One of the most common reasons for procrastination is the fear of failure. When a task is important or there is a lot at stake, the fear of not meeting expectations can be paralyzing, leading to procrastination as a way of avoiding potential disappointment or criticism.

Perfectionism: Perfectionists often procrastinate because they fear that their work won't be good enough. This can lead them to delay starting a task until they feel they can do it perfectly.

Lack of Interest: If a task is viewed as boring or unpleasant, there might be little motivation to get it done, leading to procrastination.

Overwhelm: Feeling overwhelmed by a task's scope or complexity can lead to procrastination. This often happens when a task is not well-defined or the path to completion seems too difficult or unclear.

Poor Time Management: Without effective time management skills, it's easy to underestimate how long a task will take, leading to last-minute rushes and increased procrastination.

Strategies to Combat Procrastination

To overcome procrastination, it's important to develop strategies that address the underlying reasons for delaying tasks.

Break Tasks Into Smaller Steps: Large or complex tasks can be daunting. Breaking them into smaller, manageable parts can reduce overwhelm and make the task seem more achievable. Completing these smaller tasks can provide a sense of progress and momentum.

Set Clear Goals and Deadlines: Clearly defined goals and firm deadlines can enhance focus and motivation. Use a planner or digital tools to keep track of deadlines and set reminders.

Create a Structured Schedule: Allocate specific times in your schedule for working on tasks you tend to put off. Treat these time blocks as fixed appointments.

Use Rewards and Penalties: Motivate yourself by setting up rewards for completing tasks and penalties for procrastination. For instance, reward yourself with a treat or a break after completing a task, or deny yourself a pleasurable activity if you fail to progress.

Improve Your Environment: Modify your environment to reduce distractions that lead to procrastination. This might involve cleaning up your workspace, using apps to block distracting websites, or setting up a work area that is conducive to focus.

Focus on Starting Rather Than Finishing: The thought of completing a task can be overwhelming. Shift your focus to starting the task; once you've started, it's often easier to keep going.

Understand the Consequences: Reflect on the consequences of not completing the task. Considering the negative outcomes can provide a sense of urgency and motivate you to act.

Seek Support: Share your goals with friends or colleagues who can provide support and hold you accountable. Sometimes, just knowing that others are aware of your tasks can increase your commitment to completing them.

Tackle Underlying Issues: If fear of failure or perfectionism is driving your procrastination, consider seeking help from a counselor or therapist who can help you address these issues.

Practice Mindfulness: Mindfulness can help you become more aware of your procrastination habits and the emotions associated with them. Practicing mindfulness can help you manage these feelings more effectively and increase your ability to focus on the present task.

Integrating Anti-Procrastination Habits

Successfully overcoming procrastination requires consistent effort to change habits and mindsets. Regular reflection on your progress and adjustments to your strategies as needed can help you develop more productive habits.

Procrastination is a complex issue that many people struggle with, but it can be managed with the right approaches. By understanding the psychological triggers of procrastination and actively using strategies to combat it, you can significantly improve your productivity and reduce the stress and anxiety associated with delayed tasks. Over time, these practices can help you develop a more proactive and purposeful approach to your work and personal life.

ᚦᚦᚦ

"The challenge of leadership is to be strong but not rude, kind but not weak, bold but not bully, thoughtful but not lazy, humble but not timid, proud but not arrogant."

THIRTEEN

DECISION MAKING AND ITS IMPACT ON LIFE

Decision making is a fundamental activity that significantly impacts every aspect of our lives. From minor choices like what to eat for breakfast to major decisions like which career path to pursue, the ability to make informed and effective decisions is crucial for leading a successful and fulfilling life.

Understanding Decision Making

Decision making involves choosing between two or more options and committing to a course of action. Effective decision making results in choices that lead to optimal outcomes based on the individual's goals and values. This process can be influenced by a range of factors including emotions, social pressures, information availability, and personal biases, making it a complex but essential skill to master.

The Impact of Decision Making

The quality of an individual's decisions can profoundly affect their life's trajectory. Good decision making can lead to improved life outcomes, such as career success, personal happiness, and financial stability. Conversely, poor decisions can lead to negative consequences like missed opportunities, chronic dissatisfaction, or financial hardships.

How to Make Informed and Effective Decisions

Making informed and effective decisions is not just about choosing what feels right at the moment; it involves deliberate strategies and considerations:

Define the Decision: Clearly identify what decision needs to be made. This involves understanding the nature of the decision, its scope, and its implications.

Gather Relevant Information: Collect as much relevant information as possible to inform your decision. This may involve researching, seeking advice from knowledgeable sources, and considering all available options.

Consider the Options: Weigh all possible options. It's important to list these alternatives and explore their potential outcomes. This step often requires critical thinking and the ability to forecast how different choices will play out in the future.

Evaluate the Risks and Benefits: Analyze the advantages and disadvantages of each option. Consider the potential impacts on your personal and professional life, including the short-term and long-term effects.

Check for Bias: Be aware of any biases that might influence your decision. These could include confirmation bias (favoring information that confirms your existing beliefs), overconfidence, or emotional decisions. Strive to remain objective and balanced in your assessment.

Make the Decision: After thorough evaluation, choose the option that best aligns with your goals, values, and the evidence you have gathered. Confidence in decision making comes from a clear understanding of why a particular choice is the best.

Implement the Decision: Put your decision into action. Effective implementation requires planning, resource allocation, and sometimes, the courage to take risks.

Evaluate the Outcome: After the decision has been made and the results are in, evaluate the outcome. This is crucial for learning from your choices and refining your decision-making skills over time. Consider what went well and what could be improved for future decisions.

Develop Decision-Making Skills: Regularly engage in activities that enhance your critical thinking, such as problem-solving tasks, strategic games like chess, or educational courses that focus on logic and reasoning.

Seek Feedback: Getting feedback from trusted peers or mentors can provide insights into the effectiveness of your decision-making process and help you improve.

Integrating Effective Decision-Making into Daily Life

Incorporating these strategies into daily life can transform how decisions are made, leading to better outcomes and increased satisfaction. Decision making is not a skill that improves overnight but develops through continuous practice and learning from past experiences.

Effective decision making is vital for personal and professional success. By understanding how to make informed choices, individuals can significantly influence their life's direction and outcomes. The ability to make well-considered decisions empowers people to take control of their destiny, minimize risks, and maximize their potential for a successful and rewarding life.

ϷϷϷ

"In the symphony of your life, creativity is the
melody that keeps the music playing. With each
note of creativity, you compose the unique score of
your existence."

ᐅᐅᐅ

FOURTEEN

ADAPTING TO CHANGE

Change is an inevitable part of life, affecting all aspects of our personal and professional environments. Being able to adapt effectively is crucial for thriving in an ever-evolving world. Developing resilience to change not only helps individuals manage and overcome challenges but also provides opportunities for growth and innovation.

Understanding the Nature of Change

Change can be rapid or gradual and can come in various forms—technological advancements, shifts in the economy, changes in social norms, or personal transitions such as moving to a new city or changing careers. Regardless of its form, change challenges our routines and demands a response. How we respond can significantly impact our success and well-being.

Strategies to Adapt and Thrive in Changing Environments

To successfully adapt to change, individuals need to develop strategies that enable them to cope with uncertainty and leverage new opportunities. Here are key strategies to help navigate through change effectively:

Cultivate a Positive Mindset: View change as an opportunity for growth rather than a threat. A positive attitude can reduce fear and resistance, making it easier to adapt. Embrace the mindset that change is a part of life and consider what benefits it might bring, such as learning new skills or improving existing ones.

Stay Informed: Knowledge is power. Stay updated with new developments in your field or any area affecting your life. Understanding the factors driving change can make it less intimidating and help you make more informed decisions about how to respond.

Develop Flexibility: Being flexible with your plans and expectations allows you to respond more effectively to change. Flexibility helps in adjusting strategies or goals as new information and circumstances arise.

Strengthen Your Skill Set: Continuous learning is key in a rapidly changing world. Regularly updating your skills can prepare you for unexpected changes and make you more adaptable. Consider cross-training to gain skills in multiple areas or pursuing education that enhances your adaptability.

Build a Support Network: Having a robust support system can provide emotional comfort and practical advice during times of change. Cultivate relationships with family, friends, and colleagues who can offer support. Professional networks can also provide insights and opportunities that help you adapt.

Practice Resilience: Building resilience is essential for dealing with change. Resilience can be developed through experiences that test your ability to cope and through deliberate practices like mindfulness and stress management techniques.

Plan for Multiple Outcomes: Instead of planning for a single outcome, consider various possible scenarios and develop contingency plans. This approach can reduce anxiety about the future and equip you to handle different possibilities.

Take Proactive Steps: Rather than reacting to change as it happens, take proactive steps to shape outcomes. This might involve initiating changes yourself before external circumstances force you to adapt.

Reflect and Learn from Experiences: After adapting to a new change, take time to reflect on what you learned from the experience. What worked well? What could have been done differently? Reflection enhances your ability to manage future changes more effectively.

Maintain Your Well-being: Change can be stressful, so it's important to look after your physical and emotional health. Engage in activities that you enjoy and that relax you, maintain social contacts, and ensure you get enough rest and exercise.

Integrating Adaptability into Daily Life

Integrating these strategies into daily life can help individuals prepare for and adapt to changes more fluidly. Adaptability is not an inherent trait but a skill that can be developed with practice and intentionality.

The ability to adapt to change is a critical skill that can determine how successfully individuals navigate both minor disruptions and major transitions. By embracing change as an integral part of life and preparing for it proactively, individuals can not only survive but thrive in changing environments. This adaptability not only improves personal resilience and satisfaction but also enhances professional capabilities and opportunities.

❧❧❧

"Every moment of mindfulness counts, adding up to a lifetime of peace and presence. The practice of being present is the practice of living life to its fullest."

ﭘﭘﭘ

FIFTEEN

THE SCIENCE OF HAPPINESS

Happiness is a state of well-being that encompasses living a good life, one with a sense of meaning and deep satisfaction. Understanding the science behind happiness can help us navigate the complexities of moods, feelings, and how we can foster greater happiness in our lives.

Understanding Happiness

Happiness is often defined in terms of pleasure and contentment, but it is also deeply intertwined with how meaningful we find our activities and our overall satisfaction with life. Psychologists have studied various aspects of happiness, dividing it into two broad categories: hedonic happiness (related to the presence of pleasure and absence of pain) and eudaimonic happiness (related to living in accordance with one's true self and fulfilling one's potential).

Exploring What Happiness Means

The meaning of happiness can vary significantly from person to person and culture to culture. For some, happiness might be found in the accumulation of wealth and material possessions, while for others, it is more about relationships and personal fulfillment. Research in positive psychology has often focused on what conditions support happiness, such as:

Positive Emotions: Experiencing positive emotions – joy, pride, contentment, and gratitude, among others – contributes to an overall sense of happiness.

Engagement: Activities that meet our need for engagement flush us with pleasure and can lead to deep satisfaction. This is often referred to as being in "flow," a state of immersion in which time seems to stand still.

Relationships: Humans are social creatures, and relationships provide support, enrich our lives, and contribute to our happiness.

Meaning: Having a purpose in life gives us a sense of direction and informs our daily actions, contributing to overall happiness.

Achievement: Goals give us direction and a sense of accomplishment that leads to happiness.

How to Increase Happiness in Your Life

Increasing happiness often involves tuning into these factors and finding ways to incorporate them into your daily life. Here are some strategies:

Cultivate Gratitude: Regularly take time to reflect on what you're grateful for. Studies show that gratitude is closely linked with happiness, as acknowledging the good in your life can help maintain a positive outlook.

Foster Connections: Invest time and energy in building relationships. Close connections with family and friends provide love, meaning, support, and increase our feelings of self-worth.

Engage More Deeply: Engage in activities that challenge your skills and abilities. Seek out tasks that activate a state of flow.

Find Purpose: Engage in activities that are meaningful to you. Whether through professional work, volunteer activities, or hobbies, find ways to contribute to something bigger than yourself.

Practice Optimism: Optimism is associated with better health and a higher level of happiness. Practice seeing the best in situations and cultivating a hopeful view of the future.

Take Care of Your Body: Physical well-being helps to improve mental well-being. Regular exercise, adequate sleep, and proper nutrition can raise your baseline levels of happiness.

Mindfulness and Meditation: These practices help you stay present and fully engage with your life. They reduce stress and increase overall emotional well-being.

Reduce Negative Emotions: Learning to manage and reduce your negative emotions – anger, anxiety, jealousy, and sadness – can help increase your overall happiness.

Set Manageable Goals: Set realistic goals that you can steadily work towards. Achieving goals gives a profound sense of accomplishment and satisfaction.

Laugh More: Laughter releases dopamine in the brain, which enhances your mood and relieves stress. Finding humor in daily life can elevate your spirit and make you more resilient.

Integrating Happiness into Daily Life

Integrating these elements into your daily routine can help build a happier and more satisfying life. Happiness is not just a series of happy events, but a combination of how well you feel on a day-to-day basis and how satisfied you are with your life. It is less about a fleeting state and more about cultivating habits that foster long-term well-being.

Happiness is a complex, multifaceted experience that can deeply influence our lives. By understanding the elements that contribute to our happiness and actively incorporating practices that enhance these elements, we can all lead richer, more fulfilling lives.

ᐅᐅᐅ

"Resilience is built through a thousand failures,
each teaching a lesson, each pushing you closer to
success. Embrace each failure as a step forward, not
backward."

ᗷᗷᗷ

SIXTEEN

DEVELOPING A GROWTH MINDSET

A growth mindset is a psychological concept developed by psychologist Carol Dweck, which posits that individuals can grow their abilities and intelligence through effort, learning, and persistence. Unlike a fixed mindset, where abilities are seen as static and unchangeable, a growth mindset embraces challenges, perseveres through obstacles, sees effort as a path to mastery, and learns from criticism. This mindset is crucial for personal and professional development, as it empowers individuals to strive for growth rather than fear failure.

Understanding a Growth Mindset

The concept of a growth mindset is rooted in the belief that skills and intelligence can be developed through dedication and hard work. This idea breeds a love for learning and a resilience that is essential for great accomplishment. Individuals with a growth mindset view challenges as opportunities to improve, not as insurmountable obstacles.

Challenges: Those with a growth mindset embrace challenges, seeing them as opportunities to learn and grow rather than threats that could lead to failure.

Obstacles: Instead of giving up when faced with obstacles, individuals with a growth mindset persist, showing resilience and determination.

Effort: Effort is seen as a necessary path to mastery. It is not something to be avoided; instead, it's something to be embraced as a way to learn and improve.

Criticism: Constructive criticism is valued because it is viewed as a source of information that can help improve performance, not as a personal attack.

Success of Others: Instead of feeling threatened by the success of others, people with a growth mindset find lessons and inspiration in the success of others.

Shifting to a Growth Mindset

Adopting a growth mindset involves changing fundamental beliefs about learning and intelligence. Here are strategies to help cultivate a growth mindset:

Acknowledge and Embrace Imperfections: Hiding from your weaknesses means you'll never overcome them. Acknowledge your flaws and turn them into opportunities for growth.

View Challenges as Opportunities: Each challenge is an opportunity to grow stronger and smarter. Instead of avoiding challenges, embrace them eagerly.

Try Different Learning Tactics: There's no one-size-fits-all model for learning. What works for one person might not work for another. Experiment with different learning techniques and strategies to find what works best for you.

Follow the Research on Brain Plasticity: The human brain is constantly changing in response to our experiences. By understanding that the brain is like a muscle that can be strengthened through use, our fundamental approach to learning and intelligence changes.

Replace the Word "Failing" with "Learning": When you make a mistake or fall short of a goal, you haven't failed; you've learned. This perspective helps you try again more intelligently.

Stop Seeking Approval: When you prioritize approval over learning, you sacrifice your own potential for growth. Focus on what you are learning, not on how you are performing.

Value the Process Over the End Result: The focus should be on the process of growth, not on the outcome. Reward effort, strategy, and progress, not just the end result.

Cultivate Grit: Grit is passion and perseverance for long-term and meaningful goals. It is the ability to persist in something you feel passionate about and persevere when you face obstacles.

Encourage Constructive Criticism: Learn to hear and embrace constructive criticism. Use it as feedback to improve, rather than as a reason to get discouraged or give up.

Use the Word "Yet": Dweck suggests that just adding the word "yet" when facing obstacles can help overcome self-limiting beliefs. For instance, instead of saying "I can't do this," say, "I can't do this yet."

Integrating Growth Mindset into Daily Life

Incorporating a growth mindset into everyday life means being mindful of your attitudes and responses to situations that typically challenge you. Reflect on your experiences daily, focusing on what you learned and how you can continue to develop. Regular reflection can reinforce a growth mindset and help you become more resilient to the setbacks that are part of any worthwhile endeavor.

Developing a growth mindset is a transformative process that changes how individuals perceive challenges and obstacles. By adopting and nurturing a growth mindset, you can open up endless possibilities for personal growth and achievement, leading to a more successful and fulfilling life.

𝒫𝒫𝒫

"In a world full of change, the learners shall inherit
the earth, while the learned will find themselves
beautifully equipped to deal with a world that no
longer exists."

ᗞᗞᗞ

SEVENTEEN
SELF-CARE: TAKING CARE OF YOUR MIND AND BODY

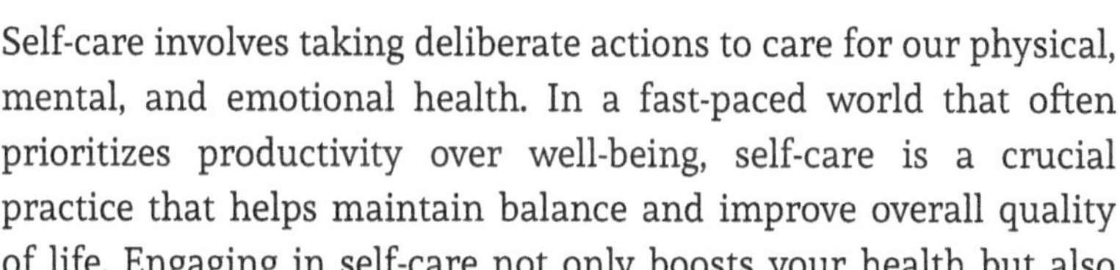

Self-care involves taking deliberate actions to care for our physical, mental, and emotional health. In a fast-paced world that often prioritizes productivity over well-being, self-care is a crucial practice that helps maintain balance and improve overall quality of life. Engaging in self-care not only boosts your health but also enhances your effectiveness in handling the demands of daily life.

Understanding the Importance of Self-Care

Self-care is essential for building resilience against the stressors of life. It enables you to recharge your batteries and can prevent burnout. When you take care of your mind and body, you're better equipped to live your best life. Self-care practices promote a healthier, more sustainable lifestyle, allowing you to maintain your health and improve your mood, which in turn can positively affect your relationships and productivity.

Physical Self-Care

Physical self-care includes activities that help you stay fit and maintain good physical health. These activities may involve exercise, proper diet, sufficient sleep, and regular medical check-ups. Here are some practical tips for implementing physical self-care:

Regular Exercise: Engage in regular physical activity tailored to your preferences and needs. Exercise not only improves physical health but also boosts mental health by releasing endorphins, natural mood lifters.

Balanced Diet: Eat a balanced diet rich in fruits, vegetables, lean proteins, and whole grains to fuel your body with the nutrients it needs to function optimally. Avoid excessive intake of processed foods, sugar, and saturated fats.

Adequate Sleep: Ensure you get enough sleep each night. Sleep is crucial for physical health, emotional well-being, and cognitive function. Establish a soothing bedtime routine and try to go to bed and wake up at the same time every day.

Hydration: Drinking enough water each day is critical for maintaining health. Hydration is essential for digestion, circulation, absorption of nutrients, and even skin health.

Regular Medical Care: Keep up with regular medical check-ups, including visits to your primary care provider, dentist, and other necessary medical professionals. Preventative care can catch problems before they become serious.

Mental and Emotional Self-Care

Mental and emotional self-care involves practices that help reduce stress and improve your mental health and emotional well-being. Here are strategies to help nurture your mental and emotional health:

Mindfulness and Meditation: Practices like mindfulness and meditation can reduce stress and anxiety, enhance concentration, and promote a general sense of well-being.

Limit Screen Time: Excessive use of screens, especially social media, can lead to increased feelings of anxiety and inadequacy. Set limits on your screen time, particularly before bedtime.

Journaling: Writing down your thoughts and feelings can be a therapeutic activity, helping you understand and manage your emotions more effectively.

Therapy and Counseling: Seeking professional help when needed is a vital aspect of self-care. Therapists can provide support and tools to deal with mental health issues like depression and anxiety.

Relaxation Techniques: Learn and practice relaxation techniques such as deep breathing exercises, progressive muscle relaxation, or yoga. These practices can help decrease stress and improve your sense of well-being.

Social Self-Care

Social interactions are a fundamental aspect of self-care. They can significantly affect mental and emotional health:

Quality Time with Loved Ones: Spend time with family and friends who uplift and support you. Positive social interactions can boost feelings of belonging and purpose.

Setting Boundaries: It's important to set boundaries to protect your energy. Know when to say no, and don't overcommit yourself.

Community Involvement: Engage in community activities or groups that align with your interests or values. Being part of a community can reduce feelings of loneliness and increase your sense of belonging.

Integrating Self-Care into Everyday Life

Incorporating self-care into your daily routine might seem daunting at first, but it's about making small changes and setting realistic goals. Prioritize activities that are most beneficial to you and remember that self-care is a personal matter—what works for others might not work for you.

Self-care is not selfish; it is necessary. Regularly engaging in self-care practices can help maintain and improve your overall health, enhance your productivity, and enrich your experience of life. By taking care of your mind and body, you can better care for others and meet the challenges of your daily life more effectively.

ppp

"Setting a goal is not the main thing. It is deciding
how you will go about achieving it and staying
with that plan."

ᐳᐳᐳ

EIGHTEEN

BREAKING BAD HABITS

Bad habits—actions or behaviors that are detrimental to one's physical, mental, or emotional well-being—are often ingrained responses that develop through repeated exposure to certain cues and rewards. Breaking these habits is crucial for improving quality of life and achieving personal growth. Understanding how to effectively identify and overcome these habits is a key component of self-improvement.

Understanding Habits

Habits are automated behaviors that are triggered by contextual cues: situations, feelings, or thoughts that prompt us to act in certain ways without much conscious deliberation. This automation makes habits incredibly efficient but also difficult to break, especially when they provide immediate rewards or relief.

Identifying Bad Habits

The first step in breaking bad habits is to identify them clearly. This process involves self-awareness and may require you to:

Keep a Habit Journal: Track your daily activities and note habits that could be detrimental to your well-being. Document the context in which the habit occurs, including the time of day, preceding events, and how you feel before, during, and after the habit.

Seek Feedback: Sometimes it's difficult to recognize one's own bad habits. Feedback from friends, family, or colleagues can provide insights into behaviors you may not notice.

Assess the Impact: Consider how the habit affects your life. Does it harm your health, waste your time, or prevent you from achieving your goals? Understanding the consequences can motivate you to make a change.

Techniques for Breaking Bad Habits

Once you've identified a bad habit, you can use several strategies to break it:

Understand the Habit Loop: Each habit consists of a cue, a routine, and a reward. Understanding these components can help you dismantle the habit. Identify the cue that triggers the habit, the routine you perform, and the reward you receive from it.

Change the Environment: Altering your environment to remove cues associated with bad habits can significantly increase your chances of success. If you habitually snack while watching TV, try rearranging your seating so that snacks are not within easy reach.

Replace the Habit with a Positive One: Instead of trying to stop a habit cold turkey, replace it with a healthier alternative that addresses the same cue and provides a similar reward. For instance, if you bite your nails when you're nervous, try squeezing a stress ball instead.

Use the "If-Then" Technique: Plan your response in advance: "If X happens, then I will do Y." For example, "If I feel the urge to smoke, then I will take a brisk walk instead." This planning can help you deal with temptation systematically.

Focus on Small Changes: Trying to change too much at once can be overwhelming and counterproductive. Focus on breaking one habit at a time or breaking down the habit into manageable parts.

Increase Your Motivation: Write down the reasons why you want to break the habit and keep them visible. Continuously remind yourself of the benefits you will enjoy by breaking the habit.

Set Clear Goals and Track Your Progress: Setting specific, measurable, achievable, relevant, and time-bound (SMART) goals can provide clear benchmarks for success. Keep a record of your progress to maintain motivation and accountability.

Get Support: Share your goal of breaking a bad habit with supportive friends or family who can provide encouragement and hold you accountable.

Practice Mindfulness: Being more aware of your thoughts and feelings can help you manage the impulses that drive bad habits. Mindfulness meditation can be particularly effective in strengthening your ability to control your actions.

Be Patient and Persistent: Breaking habits doesn't happen overnight. It often requires repeated efforts and can involve setbacks. Be patient with yourself and persistent in your efforts.

Integrating New Behaviors

Successfully breaking a bad habit involves not only stopping the unwanted behavior but also establishing new patterns that are beneficial. This integration phase is crucial and requires consistent practice until the new behavior becomes as automatic as the old one was.

Breaking bad habits is a challenging but essential process for personal development and health. It requires an understanding of the behaviors and their triggers, a strategic plan for change, and a commitment to continuous effort and adjustment. By applying these techniques, you can replace destructive patterns with constructive ones, leading to lasting changes and a healthier lifestyle.

ᗞᗞᗞ

"Emotional intelligence is perhaps the most precious currency of human interactions, buying us deeper relationships and more fulfilling interactions."

ᗧᗧᗧ

NINETEEN

THE ROLE OF CREATIVITY IN SELF-EXPRESSION

Creativity plays a pivotal role in self-expression, offering a unique conduit through which individuals can explore and articulate their innermost feelings, thoughts, and experiences. It serves as a fundamental mechanism for growth, allowing for personal exploration and the development of a deeper connection with oneself and others. Engaging in creative activities can significantly enhance mental health and overall well-being by providing a therapeutic outlet for stress, fostering a sense of accomplishment, and facilitating personal insight and self-awareness.

Understanding Creativity and Self-Expression

Creativity involves generating new ideas, making connections between existing ideas, or developing innovative solutions to problems. It is not confined to artistic pursuits alone but is a valuable skill in many aspects of life. Self-expression through creativity can take many forms, from writing and painting to cooking and gardening. It provides a powerful means for individuals to convey their personal identity, experiences, and emotions.

The Benefits of Creative Expression

Emotional Release: Creative expression offers an outlet for conveying feelings that might be difficult to articulate verbally. This release can provide a therapeutic effect, helping individuals process complex emotions and alleviate stress.

Self-Discovery: Engaging in creative activities can lead to greater self-understanding. As individuals create, they may uncover emotions, desires, and aspects of their identities that were previously unexamined or suppressed.

Cognitive Flexibility: Creativity encourages thinking in non-linear ways, enhancing problem-solving skills and cognitive flexibility. This kind of flexible thinking can lead to better adaptation to life's challenges and changes.

Improved Mental Health: Studies have shown that engaging in creative activities can decrease symptoms of anxiety, depression, and stress. Activities like painting, writing, or playing music can serve as a form of mindfulness, keeping individuals present and engaged in a rewarding activity.

Enhanced Communication: Creativity can be a means of communicating one's perspective to others, providing a bridge to understanding and empathy between diverse viewpoints. Through sharing creative works, individuals can connect with others on a deep emotional level.

Confidence and Identity: The process of creating and sharing one's work can build confidence and a strong sense of identity. Overcoming the challenges inherent in creative work can foster a sense of achievement and empowerment.

Strategies for Enhancing Creativity in Self-Expression

To harness the benefits of creativity for personal growth and mental health, consider the following strategies:

Dedicate Time to Creative Endeavors: Like any skill, creativity flourishes with practice. Set aside regular time to engage in creative activities, treating this time as a necessary component of your self-care routine.

Explore Different Mediums: Don't limit yourself to one form of creativity. Experiment with different mediums and activities to find what resonates with you and offers the greatest therapeutic benefit.

Create a Stimulating Environment: Arrange a physical space that inspires creativity. This might include organizing a dedicated workspace, decorating it with inspiring objects, or ensuring you have the necessary tools and materials at hand.

Use Prompts and Challenges: Sometimes, starting with a blank slate can be daunting. Use creative prompts or set yourself challenges to overcome creative blocks and stimulate new ideas.

Reflect on Your Process and Products: Spend time reflecting on both the process of creation and the end product. Consider what you learned during the process, how it made you feel, and what the finished piece says about your current state or development.

Share Your Work: Sharing your creative work can be rewarding and terrifying, but it is often an enriching experience. Feedback can provide new insights into your work and encourage further artistic and personal growth.

Join a Community: Engage with a community of like-minded individuals who share your creative interests. This can provide motivation, inspiration, and support, as well as opportunities for collaboration.

Integrating Creativity into Daily Life

Incorporating creativity into daily life involves recognizing its value not only as a leisure activity but as a vital part of enhancing life quality. Whether it's writing a journal, sketching, crafting, or playing music, each act of creation is a step toward a richer, more fulfilling life.

The role of creativity in self-expression is multifaceted, offering significant benefits for personal growth and mental health. It allows for emotional catharsis, promotes cognitive flexibility, and fosters deeper self-understanding. By actively engaging in creative expression, individuals can explore and assert their unique voices, achieve personal insight, and enhance their overall well-being.

ᗺᗺᗺ

"In the art of life, every setback is merely a setup for a comeback. Your resilience is your brush, your spirit the colors."

♡♡♡

TWENTY

INTEGRATING PSYCHOLOGICAL WISDOM INTO DAILY LIFE

Integrating psychological wisdom into daily life is about applying the principles and strategies discussed throughout this exploration to enhance personal growth, improve relationships, and increase overall well-being. By understanding and utilizing concepts from various psychological disciplines, individuals can lead more fulfilling, productive, and balanced lives.

Summarizing Key Psychological Principles

Self-Empowerment: Understanding that you have the ability to influence your own life outcomes is crucial. Embrace self-motivation, overcome fears, and persistently pursue personal goals.

Resilience: Building resilience is essential for coping with adversity. This involves maintaining a positive outlook, managing emotions effectively, and viewing challenges as opportunities for growth.

Positive Thinking: Cultivating a positive mindset can significantly affect your emotional and physical well-being. Focus on nurturing optimistic thoughts and engaging in behaviors that enhance positivity.

Emotional Intelligence: Developing emotional intelligence improves interpersonal relationships and self-understanding. This involves recognizing and managing your own emotions and effectively interacting with others.

Goal Setting and Achievement: Setting clear, achievable goals is fundamental for success. Employ strategies to ensure these goals are aligned with your values and provide a roadmap for personal and professional growth.

Creativity and Self-Expression: Engaging in creative activities facilitates self-expression and promotes mental health. This not only enriches your life but also allows you to communicate and connect with others more deeply.

Mindfulness: Practicing mindfulness enhances your presence and awareness, allowing for better concentration, reduced stress, and a deeper appreciation for the present moment.

Handling Change: Adapting to change is a necessary skill in a rapidly evolving world. Develop flexibility and openness to new experiences to effectively manage and respond to change.

Understanding Happiness: Recognize that happiness is derived from a combination of engaging in meaningful activities, fostering relationships, and achieving personal goals. Strive to balance pleasure and purpose in your life.

Breaking Bad Habits: Identify and modify or replace habits that hinder your personal growth. Implement strategies that foster healthier behaviors and thought patterns.

Applying Psychological Wisdom Every Day

To effectively integrate these principles into daily life, consider the following strategies:

Daily Reflection: Take time each day to reflect on your experiences and feelings. Use a journal to document your thoughts, successes, and areas where you can improve. This practice can enhance self-awareness and guide personal growth.

Routine Practice: Incorporate psychological strategies into your daily routine. For example, start your day with a mindfulness exercise, use positive affirmations, or set daily goals that align with your long-term objectives.

Continuous Learning: Keep yourself informed about psychological research and insights that can enhance your understanding of yourself and others. This could involve reading books, attending workshops, or participating in educational courses.

Seek Feedback: Regularly seek feedback from trusted peers or mentors. This can provide you with different perspectives and help refine your approach to personal development.

Foster Relationships: Make a conscious effort to strengthen your relationships through better communication, empathy, and emotional sharing. Relationships are vital for emotional support and happiness.

Adapt Flexibly: Be open to change and willing to adjust your methods and strategies as necessary. Flexibility is key to responding effectively to life's unpredictable challenges.

Self-Care: Prioritize self-care by ensuring that you maintain a healthy balance between work and personal life. Engage in physical activities, eat well, and get enough rest.

Use Psychological Tools: Apply tools like cognitive-behavioral techniques to manage negative thoughts and behaviors. Utilize relaxation techniques to manage stress and enhance mental clarity.

Community Involvement: Engage with communities that support your growth. This could be professional networks, social groups, or online communities focused on personal development.

Teach Others: Share your knowledge and experiences with others. Teaching is a powerful way to deepen your own understanding and to help others on their personal growth journeys.

Integrating Into Daily Life

Integrating psychological wisdom into your daily life is a dynamic and continuous process that requires intention, practice, and commitment. By actively applying these principles, you can improve your ability to handle life's challenges, enhance your relationships, and achieve a deeper sense of fulfillment and well-being. Each day offers a new opportunity to apply this knowledge and to live a more enriched and meaningful life.

ppp

"A positive mindset brings inner peace, strength, and endless possibilities. Cultivate it with care and watch your life transform."

♡♡♡

TWENTY-ONE
SUMMARY

In our journey through the nuanced realms of psychological wisdom and personal empowerment, we have explored a comprehensive array of strategies aimed at enhancing individual growth and improving mental health. Each chapter has delved into different aspects of personal development, offering insights and practical advice to help readers navigate the complex landscape of their inner lives and external interactions. This summary chapter encapsulates the key concepts discussed, highlighting how these ideas can be interwoven into a cohesive approach to living a more fulfilled and empowered life.

Empowering the Self

The foundational concept of self-empowerment underscores the entire discussion. Recognizing and nurturing one's intrinsic power to effect change is vital. This involves a deep dive into understanding one's strengths and weaknesses, setting achievable goals, and maintaining a growth-oriented mindset that cherishes progress and learning over perfection. Empowerment is not just about reaching heights in professional or social settings; it's about cultivating a profound sense of self-worth and capability.

Building Resilience

Resilience has been a recurring theme, emphasizing its importance in facing life's adversities. Developing resilience is not merely about recovering from setbacks; it is about using challenges as springboards for growth. Techniques such as maintaining a positive outlook, engaging in regular self-reflection, and cultivating emotional intelligence play crucial roles in enhancing one's capacity to adapt and thrive in the face of difficulties.

Harnessing the Power of Positive Thinking

The power of positive thinking can significantly alter one's approach to life. By focusing on positive outcomes and maintaining an optimistic view, individuals can improve their mental well-being and overall life satisfaction. This does not mean ignoring the complexities and challenges of life but rather choosing to approach them with a mindset that favors constructive outcomes.

Enhancing Emotional Intelligence

Emotional intelligence is critical for effective personal and professional interactions. It involves more than just managing one's emotions; it extends to understanding and empathizing with others, which enhances communication and strengthens relationships. Improving emotional intelligence through mindfulness, empathy exercises, and active listening can lead to more meaningful connections and successful interactions.

Setting and Achieving Goals

Effective goal setting is a skill that drives personal and professional development. By setting clear, measurable, and realistic goals, individuals can create a sense of direction and purpose. This process involves not only identifying end goals but also appreciating and rewarding the small steps achieved along the journey.

The Role of Creativity in Self-Expression

Creativity serves as a vital outlet for self-expression and is essential for mental health. It allows individuals to explore and articulate feelings and thoughts that might be stifled otherwise. Engaging in creative activities can provide emotional release, foster problem-solving skills, and enhance one's sense of identity.

Practicing Mindfulness

Mindfulness and presence are powerful practices that enhance one's mental focus and emotional clarity. By cultivating mindfulness, individuals can improve their ability to concentrate, reduce stress levels, and enjoy a more peaceful and productive life.

Adapting to Change

Change is inevitable, and the ability to adapt is crucial for sustained success and happiness. Strategies for adapting to change include embracing a flexible mindset, staying informed about changes, and being proactive rather than reactive.

Understanding Happiness

Happiness is a multifaceted aspect of life that stems from engaging in meaningful activities, fostering positive relationships, and achieving personal goals. It is influenced by a complex interplay of psychological factors, and understanding these can lead to a more joyful and satisfying life.

Breaking Bad Habits

Identifying and altering detrimental habits is essential for personal growth. Techniques for breaking bad habits include understanding the habit loop, replacing undesirable habits with beneficial ones, and using strategies to make new habits stick.

Integrating Psychological Wisdom into Daily Life

The ultimate goal of exploring these psychological concepts is to integrate them into everyday living. This involves regular practice, continual learning, and a commitment to applying these principles in various life situations. By weaving psychological wisdom into the fabric of daily activities, individuals can enhance their ability to handle challenges, improve relationships, and lead richer, more rewarding lives.

The journey through the landscape of psychological wisdom and personal empowerment is ongoing and dynamic. It requires dedication, awareness, and the willingness to continuously adapt and grow. Each chapter of our exploration offers tools and insights that, when applied, can profoundly transform one's life. This summary not only highlights the interconnectedness of these concepts but also reaffirms the importance of each in building a balanced, empowered, and fulfilled life.

ㅂㅂㅂ

Citation And References

This book represents the culmination of extensive research and meticulous analysis, incorporating a diverse range of sources, including numerous books, scholarly studies, and personal experiences. Additionally, I have scoured various websites to gather relevant information and data essential for the compilation of this work. I have taken every precaution to ensure the accuracy of the information presented and have diligently cited all sources to acknowledge their contributions.

Despite these efforts, the possibility of inadvertent errors remains. I deeply value the insights of my readers and appreciate any feedback that can help identify and rectify such inaccuracies. I encourage you to bring any discrepancies to my attention.

Your feedback is not only welcome but crucial, as it will aid in correcting current editions and enhancing the content of future ones. I am committed to maintaining the highest standards of accuracy and reliability in my work and thank you for your support and understanding.

Additionally, I firmly uphold the principle of freedom of speech and expression as guaranteed under Article 19(1)(a) of the Constitution of India, and I respect the diverse viewpoints and expressions of all readers.

ppp

Other Books Of The Author

1. Empowering Minds: A Journey into Women's Self-Discovery and Power
2. The Dynamics of Motivation: Catalyzing Thought into Action
3. Meditation and Mental Well Being: The Path to Inner Peace and Clarity
4. The Psychology of Child Education: Nurturing Future Generations
5. Ethical Enlightenment: A Modern Guide to Living with Integrity
6. Voices of Empowerment: Stories of Women Rising Against Odds
7. Social Psychology in Everyday Life: Understanding Human Connections
8. The Essence of Motivational Speaking: Inspiring Change in Others
9. Balancing Acts: Women, Work, and the Will to Lead
10. Guiding with Grace: Raising Children with Compassion and Awareness
11. The Power of Positive Aging: Embracing Life After Fifty
12. Building Resilient Communities: Social Work in Action
13. The Ethical Educator: Principles for Teaching and Learning
14. From Insight to Impact: Social Psychology for a Better World
15. The Ethics of Empathy: A Guide to Ethical Living
16. The Science of Empowering the Self: Navigating Life's Challenges with Psychological Wisdom
17. The Mindful Conscious Leader: Meditation Techniques for Modern Management
18. Pioneering Spirit: Women's Pathways to Leadership and Empowerment
19. Feeling to Healing: The Role of Emotional Intelligence in Child Development
20. Transformative Talks and Words of Inspiration: Insights into Motivational Oratory

❧❧❧

Contact

Dr. Minakshi Bansal
Social Activist
Ahmedabad, Gujarat, Bharat
minakshiindiag20@yahoo.com

❦❦❦

|| LOKAHA SAMASTHAHA SUKHINO BHAVANTU ||

• 131 •